Scale an Automated Online Business

Scale an Automated Online Business: Unlocking and Perfecting Profitability

John A. Estrella

Scale an Automated Online Business:
Unlocking and Perfecting Profitability

Paperback: 978-1-990135-03-3
Kindle: 978-1-990135-04-0
Audible: 978-1-990135-05-7

Editing by Suzanne Baal
Cover design by Luisito Pangilinan

Agilitek Corporation
Markham, Ontario, Canada

agilitek.com

About the Author

John A. Estrella, PhD, CMC, PMP, coaches solopreneurs how to start, scale, and sell profitable automated online businesses using proven strategies and systems. He consistently strives to realize more and higher achievements. With a proven track record of working with creativity, integrity, and drive, he earns respect, inspires cooperation, and exceeds expectations.

Dr. Estrella founded consulting and online companies. He currently serves as the Academic Coordinator of the Project Management Certificate at The Chang School of Continuing Education at Ryerson University. He contributes to the community as Scouts Canada's International Commissioner. He was recognized with the Queen Elizabeth II Diamond Jubilee Medal for his volunteer work with Canada's youth.

His educational background includes a BSc (Dean's List) and an MSc (Teaching Fellow & Scholar; 4.0 GPA) degrees in Computer Science. The Project Management Institute (PMI) Educational Foundation awarded him a scholarship for his PhD in Organization and Management (4.0 GPA). Continuing education includes Conversational French (Toronto) and Nonprofit Board (Harvard).

Connect with Dr. Estrella at https://johnestrella.com.

Automated Online Business Books

Start an Automated Online Business: Turning Your Passions Into Millions

Paperback: 978-1-990135-00-2
Kindle: 978-1-990135-01-9
Audible: 978-1-990135-02-6

Scale an Automated Online Business: Unlocking and Perfecting Profitability

Paperback: 978-1-990135-03-3
Kindle: 978-1-990135-04-0
Audible: 978-1-990135-05-7

Sell an Automated Online Business: Maximizing the Selling Price

Paperback: 978-1-990135-06-4
Kindle: 978-1-990135-07-1
Audible: 978-1-990135-08-8

Solopreneur Programs

Apply to our programs by visiting our website.
https://agilitek.com/solopreneur

Dedication

To my wife, Maria, and my children, Joshua, Jacob, and Clara, this book is dedicated to all of you.

—John A. Estrella

Table of Contents

Preface

After clicking on so many online ads for free checklists, presentations, and webinars, I got so frustrated for wasting so much of my time.

First, several of them present shallow and regurgitated materials. There is no breadth and depth. They experienced some success applying a technique that they learned somewhere from someone, and they expect that you will be able to replicate their success. With a rented Lamborghini in the background, they attempt to project an image of success. Second, they only focus on one aspect of the problem, not the end-to-end process of running a thriving business. Third, their companies do not necessarily contribute to significant and long-lasting value for their clients. They are selling bandages, knowing that their customers need surgery.

My view of a business is different. While some entrepreneurs like to build a business that will become a public company someday, I want to start companies that will become profitable within a few months. Other entrepreneurs find thrills in hustling with investors to fund their ventures. In contrast, I like to bootstrap a company so that I can retain majority control. Several solopreneurs spend long hours running their business and creating social media content to remain in the spotlight. For me, I let my automated online business run on its own so that I can enjoy life with my family, pursue what I want, and contribute my fair share to the community.

I've decided to write a book trilogy about starting, scaling, and selling an automated online business with a desire to share with those who will listen. You cannot build a sustainable business by merely knowing how to run an incredible Facebook ad campaign. Creating content for YouTube or recording podcasts continuously to get more likes, shares, and comments will not do the trick. You need to master the entire process, and more importantly, you need to integrate them seamlessly together.

This book focuses on the second portion of the trilogy by teaching you how to scale an automated online business to unlock and perfect your company's profitability. We begin by deconstructing the value chain to optimize the end-to-end processes and clarify the focus on customer lifetime value (CLV). After that, you'll build the foundation for growth by creating a marketing war chest and building trust to increase conversions.

With the critical components in place, it's time to hyper-scale your business growth. To do so, you'll need to scale paid digital advertising and incorporate affiliate marketing. To round the growth machine, you also need to invest in evergreen traffic sources.

When you reach this point, you would have built an automated online business that can thrive without you while remaining profitable with sustainable rapid growth. It will be reasonably lucrative so that you can continue to let it run or sell it to another entrepreneur. Your venture will remain a solo operation, albeit with some part-time external help from contractors, specialists, and providers.

Thank you for joining me on this journey. I'll be your mentor. I will show you the way and steer you away from common mistakes, but you have to do the work. Reach out to me anytime at https://johnestrella.com, and I'll do my best to help you. We are on this journey together.

Even if you are intellectually smart, don't let your mindset fail you. That's the biggest challenge, which I know you can overcome. I'm counting on you. Good luck!

Acknowledgment

Dan Poynter inspired me to write my first book. Over the years, I picked up valuable entrepreneurial insights from Timothy Ferriss, Chris Guillebeau, and John Warrillow. When it comes to business strategy, I subscribed to the expertise of Alan Weiss, Mike Michalowicz, Michael E. Gerber, Richard S. Ruback, and Royce Yudkoff. I'm so thankful for their wisdom.

Behind the scenes, a mountain biker opened the door for me to achieve a business breakthrough. Never in a hundred years would I have imagined that a former bartender will show me how to put the business pieces together and that a former US Navy SEAL holds the key to sell with confidence, care, and integrity. Joined by a world-class team of mindset experts and paid advertising gurus, I was able to crack the million-dollar puzzle. They shall remain nameless for now but rest assured I owe them my sincerest gratitude.

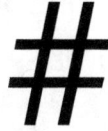

INTRODUCTION

Congratulations on your decision to grow your automated online business!

While some fortunate entrepreneurs enjoy natural growth with their business, others are not so lucky. Most people experience a decline in revenue, or their business fizzles out ultimately. If you are one of the lucky ones, even if your business is experiencing organic growth, deliberately manage the situation to maximize your gains.

Business growth comes from more revenue per product, more products, and more customers. Take note that customers were once prospects, who were once leads, who were once strangers. The more strangers who hear about your products, the more opportunities you'll have to identify them as leads. After you qualify them, they can be converted into prospects and eventually into paying customers.

It may seem simple, and it is, but several factors affect business growth trajectory, and one of them is the conversion rate. If you need to show your product to 100 people (strangers), 25 may show an interest (leads), ten may recognize that your product will meet their needs (prospects), and five may eventually buy your product (customers). These numbers provide precious insights: You need to present your product to 100 strangers to sell five products.

Suppose it costs you $1 to present your product to each stranger, and you sell your product for $60 each. The marketing cost of $100 would generate $300 in gross revenue. If the total cost of producing or delivering those products is $100, you will make a total of $100 in profit. To double your profit, assuming all things being equal, you can spend $200 to market your product, and you should expect to generate $600 in gross revenue, yielding $200 in profit.

Assuming that the conversion rate continues to be viable, your next hurdle is growth limits (processing capability, supply availability, logistics limitations, customer population, usage limits, and more). These growth limits impact physical (e.g., clothes, books, gadgets, etc.) and digital products (e.g., online courses, mobile apps, software subscriptions, etc.). You'll need to identify and address these growth limits by asking exploratory questions.

If your company gets flooded with orders, how many can be fulfilled per hour, day, week, or month based on the current capacity? Will your supplier be able to provide the materials that you need to produce your product? What's the lead time? A surge in orders is a bigger problem for a physical product, but it can also impact digital products.

For example, you may limit the number of user licenses, or perhaps your computer server can only support a certain amount of concurrent users or active accounts. For logistics, is there a maximum size or weight allowed? Even for a digital product, are there file size or type restrictions? Consider the maximum number of potential customers. Along with that, assess the inherent usage limit based on the nature of your product. For example, if you are selling a dating app, you will only sell one license per person.

Before you can scale, you must establish your business well. Otherwise, you'll just magnify problems. Having solid business foundations means that your product must solve a significant problem for someone. You should have set the price so that you can make a profit of at least ⅓ (33% or higher) for each sale (Rule of ⅓) and so that your customer will realize at least ten times the value relative to the selling price (10X Principle).

The mechanics of the Rule of ⅓ and the 10X Principle are beyond the scope of this book. If you are not familiar with these principles, please read the precursor to this book, *Start an Automated Online Business: Turning Your Passions Into Millions*. Once you have confirmed these foundations, you are ready to take your business to the next level.

To scale your business, we'll help you find the answers to the following questions:

- How does the entire value chain look for your business?
- Are you maximizing the customer lifetime value (CLV)?
- Which levers can you pull to increase revenue?
- How are you leveraging social proof and conversion rate optimization (CRO)?

Deconstructing the value chain will help you ensure that your business has a solid foundation rooted in reliable data analytics. You can remove elements that block or inhibit scalability and start delegating back-end processes. To grow, you also need to create efficiency by optimizing end-to-end processes to manage key performance indicators (KPIs), incorporate conversion rate optimization (CRO), streamline the digital footprint, manage risks, and diversify revenue.

With a solid foundation in place, your marketing efforts can maximize CLV by building trust with your customers to optimize conversions. Along the way, explore other evergreen sources of customers by incorporating affiliate marketing and paid digital advertising. Are you ready to grow your business? Let's get you growing and discuss the details of how to do all of this!

★ ★ ★ ★ ★

Please take a selfie or video with this book and share it on social media and Amazon. Feel free to tag me and keep me updated on your progress.

#solopreneur #aob-book #aob-trilogy

Thanks, John Estrella

CHAPTER 1

DECONSTRUCT THE VALUE CHAIN

If you think of your automated online business as a machine, it takes inputs, processes them, and generates outputs. With a product ready for sale, inputs include identifying potential customers, enticing them to consider your product, and then placing an order to purchase it. When a customer has placed an order, you need to deliver the product and maintain a high customer satisfaction level. Some steps in fulfilling the order include accepting payment, providing the product, welcoming the customer, responding to their questions, and resolving any issues. On the other end, outputs include a list of satisfied customers, business metrics, and, more importantly, net profit for you, the owner.

Let's use the brick-and-mortar example of a scuba diving shop to visualize the value chain. For inputs, they have a storefront on a busy street that draws passer-by and walk-in customers. They also have a website that potential customers can visit if they search for scuba diving topics. The owner also posts videos and pictures of their amazing adventures on social media channels. All of these inputs can prompt a prospective customer to visit the store.

When someone visits the store, they may look around or ask questions but not purchase anything. They may sign up for a scuba diving certification or a trip. They may also buy some products. So, there are four possible processes for this particular business. First, it's one process to answer questions. Second, when someone signs up for scuba diving certification, maybe they need access to online materials. After they complete the online training, an instructor will need to review it and schedule training dives. If the training dive requires a boat, the staff will need to book it. Third, the customer who simply booked a diving trip, assuming that they are already certified divers, will be similar but a more straightforward process. Likewise, the fourth process is also simple for someone buying a diving product.

The other end of those processes produces outputs. Respectively, we nurtured a potential customer by addressing their inquiries. Those who signed up for the certification will gain the necessary scuba diving skills and maybe need to purchase equipment or products in the future. Hopefully, those who signed up for a scuba diving trip will have a great time and return happy and tell their friends. Lastly, those who bought some gear will be satisfied and may potentially come back for more. There are several elements along the value chain, from the inputs to the processes, and finally, the outputs, but the business owner must profit in the end. So we must examine every single element of the value chain. Which ones add value, and which steps can be eliminated, optimized, automated, or delegated?

To answer these questions, we need to solidify the business foundation, collect data for analysis, remove scalability blockers, and delegate work from the back. That means looking first at the back-end processes, not the customer-facing ones, and delegating them to others. More focus can be given to serving the customers (middle of the value chain) and, more importantly, attracting them (front of the value chain).

Solidify the foundation

If your company is not yet generating at least one-third profit (Rule of ⅓) against the gross revenue, you may need to revisit your offer. Go back to the precursor book, *Start an Automated Online Business: Turning Your Passions Into Millions,* to ensure that your foundations are solid.

Are you charging enough? Are there opportunities to decrease your production cost so that you can increase your profit? If you feel that your product is already competitively priced, are you generating enough awareness? Are there other opportunities to attract more potential customers to your product? If you are getting enough prospective customers to consider your product, why are they not buying? Is it possible that you haven't communicated the real benefit of your product (10X Principle)? Are you clear on your ideal customer's problem, persona, psyche, pain, and pleasure (Five Ps)?

Without accurate data, it will be challenging to assess the company's profitability. Going back to the scuba diving shop example, if the owners don't know the number of people visiting their store, they run their business in the dark. What is the ratio of those just inquiring versus actually buying something? What's the average purchase amount? Do they know the overall profit margin? They need to have this information along with other business analytics.

Online businesses that don't know their numbers will be in the same situation. However, they have one significant advantage: they can easily capture online statistics with minimal maintenance after setting it up. Most online systems, if configured correctly, record the data automatically.

In contrast, the scuba diving shop may need to manually count the number of people coming through the door and compare that against their sales to understand the ratio of walk-ins versus buyers. Moreover, unless they ask each potential customer, they will not know how they found the dive shop. Did they see the store sign as they were driving home from work? Was it a social media post that caught their attention? If so, which one? You can see how an online business is at a distinct advantage here.

Make sure to collect data and analyze what's happening in your online business. The next section will list what you can collect and how to manage it.

Collect data for analysis

The good news about online data collection is that most of the tools are free. After you set them up, they will continue to collect data in the background without needing management or interaction. If configured correctly, you can "set it and forget it." The two primary data collection groups comprise generic analytic services such as Google Analytics and Google Search Console, and specialized measurement tools, such as Facebook Pixel.

Google Analytics is the most widely used web and app analytics service. If you haven't done so already, install it on your website and app to gain better insights into your audience. You can analyze their demographics, interests, geography, behavior, technology, and other variables. You will also be able to view how visitors get to your website and how your users use your app.

The acquisition feature will tell you which channels visitors came from, such as direct, organic search, paid search, referral, email, social, and others. You'll be able to see how your paid ads are performing and which campaigns are generating sales.

Google Search Console, another free web service for webmasters, helps index your website to make the pages visible to search engines. This service can help you find which search terms brought visitors to your website, which gives you additional insight into potential customers' priorities.

Outside of Google Analytics and Google Search Console, you need to start exploring specialized measurement tools, depending on your online footprint. Even if you are not running Facebook ads yet, make sure to install Facebook Pixel on your website. Doing so allows Facebook to track who visited your website and retarget them to bring them back. More importantly, if you are running an ad, you'll be able to pinpoint the exact ad (the specific text, image, and call to action [CTA]) that generated a particular sale.

You will likely be using a payment processor such as Stripe or PayPal, so take a close look at the data they generate and track. Examine the gross volume, net volume from sales, new customers, number of successful payments, spend per customer, dispute activity, dispute count, and high-risk charges. If you have a ticketing system such as Zendesk, take a look at the number of tickets, average response times, first reply times, and help center content. Understand their concerns and review the resolutions. Which actions led to customer satisfaction, potential repeat business, and possible referrals?

Depending on how sophisticated you want to get, several business intelligence tools or dashboard software options are available. The most important thing is to aggregate information in a way that makes sense to your business and provides you with the insights you need. You can often satisfy your needs with a simple spreadsheet by setting weekly or monthly cadence to collect, aggregate, and analyze the data. Most importantly, you need to take action based on the data.

Remove scalability blockers

Using the business analytics that you have collected, you will identify your organization's scalability blockers. We talked about delegating the back-end portion of the value chain during the automation section and then working your way forward to the front-end, customer-facing activities. In contrast, to identify the things blocking your ability to scale, you need to start from the front-end activities.

For example, if a martial arts school wants to recruit ten new members every month for the next six months, they first need to find out how many prospective members they need to meet to enroll one member. Assuming that a membership associate can close a sale at a 50% rate, she needs to talk with 20 people every month to meet the target. Further, assuming that she can speak with one person per business day, then the target is achievable.

However, if the owner wants to grow by 20 new members every month, they need to speak with 40 people. The current capacity to only talk with one person per business day is a scalability blocker. To unblock it, they need to temporarily hire another membership associate to double their capacity for the next six months or find a way to shorten the interaction so that they can speak with two people per day.

Another solution might be to improve the conversion rate to sign up three new members for every four people they speak with, resulting in a conversion rate of 75% instead of 50%. Even with just one associate, all things being equal, with this conversion rate, they'll be able to sign up 15 new members every month instead of 10.

For a dive shop that sells a spot in a boat charter, the boat's space limits their capacity. If a boat can comfortably accommodate ten divers and they want to double their revenue, they can schedule a dive charter twice, one in the morning and one in the afternoon. There might be other scalability blockers, such as the number of tanks available. There may not be enough time to refill the tanks with air between the first and second boats.

These scalability blockers also apply to online or digital products. While it's easier to visualize the scenarios with physical products, the same challenges also apply to online and digital products. For example, an influencer may sell a sponsored post on an Instagram account. To maintain the account's high-quality content, he may offer only one sponsored post per day. If he sells each sponsored post for $500, then his income ceiling will be $15,000 per month (30 days). To remove this scalability blocker, he may want to charge more, say $600 per sponsored post, to increase the monthly revenue to $18,000. Although this new monthly limit is higher, it is still a limit. To go beyond it, he may decide to post twice on the weekend to lift the scalability blocker even higher.

The SCAMPER mnemonic may help solve some of these scalability blockers. It stands for Substitute, Combine, Adapt, Modify, Put to another use, Eliminate, and Reverse. If part of your value chain requires a phone call, can you substitute a recorded voicemail instead without impacting the quality of the customer experience? Suppose a process requires an accountant to review the numbers and a manager to approve the report. Can these activities be combined by delegating the approval process to the accountant also? If physicians cannot see patients in person because of a pandemic, can they adapt by offering phone or video call consultations? If the online prequalification form lets in many tire kickers, can you modify one of the questions to filter them better?

A 3M scientist in the US, Dr. Spencer Silver, attempted to develop a super-strong adhesive. It didn't work, but 3M put it to another use as a "low-tack" adhesive, which resulted in the immensely successful Post-It Notes (or sticky note). Eliminate a step in the process if it's not adding value. If you offer a "net 30" credit term, which sometimes leads to a cash flow crunch, why not reverse the process and ask for payment when your customers place an order? Review the SCAMPER options for your business to see if one or a combination will help remove or reduce scalability blockers.

It's a tough balancing act between scaling revenue and maintaining customer satisfaction. You don't want to scale too fast and end up having more unhappy customers. At the same time, you don't want to stagnate or grow too slowly because you'll be missing opportunities, and you won't be able to help more people who need your product. Identify and deconstruct each of those scalability blockers from the front to your business's back-end processes so that you can deliberately scale faster.

Delegate from the back

As a business owner, you likely wear multiple hats. You may be the business' corporate strategist, sales director, compliance supervisor, public relations manager, quality engineer, system programmer, digital marketer, website copywriter, helpdesk support, and even janitor. If you look at your customer journey, from the first time they hear about your product to the point that they became customers, they likely interacted with at least one of those roles along the value chain.

If you are performing all or most of these roles, you are your scalability blocker. As discussed previously, you need to systematically identify and dismantle each of the functions that you currently and personally perform. Are you the best person to complete that role? Do you enjoy performing that role? If the answer is no to these questions, it's time to start delegating those roles starting from the back-end processes.

Other people may disagree, but the sales team plays an essential role. Although marketers attract prospective customers, sales professionals close the deal—if there are no sales, there is no business. If there are sales, money can solve most other problems. Use your profit to hire more sales professionals. Cash allows you to hire and retain more and better staff to solve engineering, marketing, and logistical problems within your business. You can also afford automation tools to streamline processes, provide better support, and so on.

Marketing and sales are front-end activities. Product delivery and support are somewhere in the middle. Most routine activities are back-end processes, such as payroll administration, tax remittance, system upgrades, and inventory management. Along the value chain during the customer journey, which back-end activities can be performed better by someone else? Which back-end activities do you hate doing? Document the processes and then delegate them. You can either hire someone or outsource it to a third-party. If you can fully automate them or let them run with minimal human intervention, it's even better. Use the time that you freed up to increase your company's capacity to deliver the middle activities.

For product delivery and support, do the same thing that you did for the back end activities. Hire or outsource tasks that can be performed by someone else, especially those you don't enjoy doing. This situation logically brings the next question: Should you hire or outsource the front-end processes?

The quick answer is yes, but proceed partially or slowly, as this is the part that touches your customer and is most sensitive. It could be that you are the best person to do them, and you enjoy doing them—maybe this is where your passion lies, that prompted you to start the business in the first place. However, eventually, you need to let go of most of these roles to focus on scaling your business. That's a separate role altogether.

★ ★ ★ ★ ★

If you are enjoying this book so far, can you please tell your friends about it via email or social media?

#solopreneur #aob-book #aob-trilogy

Thanks in advance, John.

CHAPTER 2

OPTIMIZE END-TO-END PROCESSES

In the previous chapter, we discussed deconstructing the value chain by solidifying the foundation, collecting data for analysis, removing scalability blockers, and delegating from the back. This chapter covers how to optimize the end-to-end processes by managing the key performance indicators (KPIs), incorporating conversion rate optimization (CRO), streamlining your digital footprint, managing risks, and diversifying revenue sources.

If you would like to double your revenue, you may need to double your website traffic. It will require deliberate effort to open additional traffic sources or expand existing sources. For example, you may perform a search engine optimization (SEO) analysis to identify how to increase traffic from organic sources. If you are not running paid ads, you may want to start with pay-per-click (PPC) campaigns. Tapping into affiliate networks is another option.

However, you may have reached the traffic limit. In that case, CRO may help you scale. If the website is currently getting 10,000 visitors per month and generating 20 sales (2%), then doubling the conversion rate to 4% will double the deals with the same traffic. In most cases, it is better to perform CRO first to increase revenue before increasing website traffic. The only caveat is that CRO takes time, many trials and errors, so it is a long-term approach instead of a quick fix. You should also know that revenue may dip when you perform CRO because when you perform A/B tests, "losers" will generate lower revenue, and "winners" will increase your conversions. Over time, you'll get better results as you identify winning combinations—and we will talk more about this a bit later.

While generating more website traffic and increasing the conversion rate will generate more revenue, the business owner can also gain more profit through efficiency by lowering operating costs and streamlining the digital footprint with consolidation and automation. Additionally, manage your business risks proactively to avoid any surprises. Lastly, revenue sources should come from multiple channels to avoid dependency on a small number of significant customers or a single community. Understanding your key performance indicators is critical to understanding the dynamics of your business.

Manage key performance indicators

To truly understand what's going on with your business, pick one overall key performance indicator (KPI) and break it down into smaller components. Because this book focuses on scaling an automated online business, let's focus on profit. Analyze your company's profit by reviewing revenue and expenses separately. From there, break down the revenue sources such as one-time vs. recurring revenue, organic website traffic, affiliate networks, paid ads, and so on. On the expenses side, break them down by fixed vs. variable, fixed monthly overhead, per-unit costs, and so on. You can then identify which data you need daily, weekly, or monthly.

With this structure in place, identify where you can get the data. Designate specific sources as the book of record. As you collect and aggregate the raw data, you can always go back to the record book if there are discrepancies. Make sure that you collect data the same way and establish the same timeframe each time. Otherwise, there will be gaps and overlaps, making it impossible to compare performance from week to week or month to month.

For example, if you collect and aggregate data weekly, follow a schedule to receive or collect the previous week's data (Sunday to Saturday) every Monday morning. For monthly data, you may want to see the last month's data on the first working day of the following month. Although there are various automation tools in the market, it is perfectly acceptable to manually complete these activities using a spreadsheet until you get comfortable collecting, aggregating, reporting, and making decisions based on the data. The benefit of using a spreadsheet is as you work through it, you see the information.

Deliberately include leading indicators as part of your metrics. Revenue amount, number of website visitors, and others are trailing indicators. You get them after the fact, and you have no way of influencing them. However, suppose you are selling a product with a reasonable lead time. In that case, you can prepare for the sales influx and perhaps even spend more on advertising to increase awareness in anticipation of a sales frenzy.

For example, if you sell baby products, note that most US births happen between July and October. August is the most popular month. If you sell weather-related products, you may notice that people buy umbrellas a week later whenever it rains for 2-3 days in a row. It's essential to tap into these data points, as they are examples of fixed leading indicators.

Lastly, you need to set thresholds and assign ownership of KPIs. For example, you may want to raise a flag if the weekly revenue dips by more than 20% for two weeks in a row compared to the weekly average. Whoever owns that KPI will investigate the anomaly, identify the root cause, and develop solutions to bring the revenue back to normal.

Depending on your business, looking at your KPIs daily might be too frequent, but you should have at minimum weekly and monthly reviews. Your KPIs can help you identify potential areas for conversion rate optimization.

Incorporate conversion rate optimization

Think of the value chain as a complex and tightly integrated machine that generates website traffic and converts visitors into customers. Starting from a search result, an affiliate link, or a paid ad, visitors arrive at a landing page. The landing page will capture their email and usher them to your product page. Behind the scenes, an automated email sequence will kick in to nurture the relationship over time. The visitor will proceed to the checkout page and then the payment confirmation page. As you can see, there are so many pieces that work in harmony to convert strangers into customers.

There are endless combinations along the value chain. You cannot possibly test all of them, so you must do your testing deliberately, efficiently, and quickly. Specialists in this area often call it A/B testing. They compare one version (A) to a slightly different version (B) to determine which one performs better. They are looking for a "champion" (or winner). After they find a champion, they continuously develop new "challengers" to see if they can beat the champ. It's incredible how a simple change in words, images, or color can make a big difference.

In some cases, things that you think should go well perform poorly. The bottom line is no one can reliably predict the winner despite incorporating best practices into the equation. So you need to conduct A/B tests and let the data guide you.

For example, you may have a button on your website that says, "Buy Now." Which button color will perform better, purple or red? Run an A/B test to find out. Will the caption "online business" perform better than "digital business"? Which one will get more clicks, a black and white picture or a color picture? Which ad gets more shares on Facebook, the one with a male or a female image? This series of tests is conversion rate optimization (CRO).

Frequently, a data visualization technique called heat mapping (heat maps) gets incorporated into CRO. Heat maps keep track of how visitors interact with a web page or an app. Based on their interactions, you can identify a "winner" by trying various combinations. That is the variation that converts better. Copywriters, designers, programmers, and marketers use multiple tools to perform CRO.

For A/B testing, standard tools for landing pages include Google Optimize, Unbounce, and Leadpages. Common A/B testing features are built-in into some services. For example, Google Ads allows you to have different combinations of headlines and descriptions. For Facebook, you can do it manually by using the same ad with a slightly different copy, image, title, and call to action. Or, you can just create multiple variations and let Facebook determine the best performing ads. Smartlook, Hotjar, and Mouseflow lead the pack for heat mapping software. Standard features include heat maps, recordings, events, funnels, comments, and surveys. Now that you know how to increase your conversion rates let's talk about efficiency.

Streamline the digital footprint

As you are building your business, it is relatively common to use different software to get the job done. Retire or replace software that you have outgrown. There may be duplicate functionalities. Regardless of the reason, always look for ways to streamline and consolidate your company's digital footprint. Doing so will likely lower your operational costs, increase system reliability, simplify internal processes, and improve your customer experience. You can then reallocate time and money to focus on growing your business.

Although there are several social media platforms, do you need to manage several of them actively? Can you just upload a video on YouTube and automatically share it to Facebook, Instagram, and TikTok using a tool like IFTTT or Zapier? Can you store your podcasts on Soundcloud and distribute them automatically to iTunes, Google Play, Spotify, and others?

There are several ways to generate traffic for your website outside of organic sources. Affiliate marketing programs should be in the mix. Be sure to stay with one provider so that you avoid paying duplicate commissions. Popular programs include CJ Affiliate, Shareasale, and ClickBank. To top up your affiliate revenue, you'll need to run paid ads.

Do you need to run paid ads on Twitter, LinkedIn, and Pinterest if Google Ads gives you access to Google, YouTube, Gmail, and Blogger? Similarly, Facebook offers access to Instagram and Messenger. Other options include content discovery, native advertising, and mobile push notification from providers such as Taboola, Outbrain, and Google Firebase. Fill your traffic pipe from primary sources first (usually Facebook and Google) and use the rest as fillers, if needed. Otherwise, you'll be running too many campaigns, which will likely cost you a fortune and take too much time to manage.

Suppose you offer an online course or a membership site. In that case, you may be running your website on WordPress, and you'll continue to extend the functionality using add-ons to manage the course content, control access, and receive payments. Before you know it, you may have MemberPress, LearnDash, WooCommerce, and MailChimp plug-ins installed along with a video subscription to Vimeo or Wistia to achieve your desired functionality. Will an integrated solution like Kajabi or Ontraport make your life easier?

You know your business better than anyone else, so always keep an eye for opportunities to streamline your digital footprint. Fewer moving pieces mean fewer failure points, an excellent introduction to the next topic—managing risks and diversifying revenue.

Manage risks and diversify revenue

From this book and its predecessor book, *Start an Automated Online Business: Turning Your Passions Into Millions*, we have advocated full control and ownership of your business. In most cases, if you are deliberate about it, it's possible. However, in certain situations, you may not have a choice but to get a license or some sort of permission from someone else. Having full control and ownership is one method for risk management and revenue diversification.

Amazon offers the most sophisticated fulfillment networks in the world. With Fulfillment by Amazon (FBA), sellers store their products in Amazon's fulfillment centers, and Amazon picks, packs, ships, and provides customer service for these products. FBA helps entrepreneurs scale their business and reach more customers. While this service is excellent for drop-shippers, Amazon owns the customer list, and the seller does not. If Amazon shuts down your online store, which happens often, your business can go from millions of dollars in revenue to zero in the blink of an eye.

Some businesses rely heavily on paid advertising. If everything is going well, the outcomes are predictable, like clockwork, and things are terrific. For example, if you spend $100 on Facebook advertising, you may make

$300 in sales. If you increase it to $200 per day, you may generate $600 in sales and so on. However, if Facebook decides to shut down your ad account, you'll lose all that traffic. So, while it is great to generate traffic from Facebook, you should make sure to diversify your traffic sources.

In contrast, an affiliate marketing program offers traffic from multiple sources. More importantly, you don't need to pay them a commission until they help you sell a product. If you don't like an affiliate marketing platform, you can always move your best-performing affiliates to another platform. The only thing that you need to watch out for is partners who may switch sides. They can start sending traffic to your competitors if you don't pay them well. So, treat them nicely and build long-term relationships.

It is reasonably common for payment processors to shut down an account because of fraudulent transactions. For the most part, assuming that you are running a legitimate online business, you have no control over it. An unscrupulous competitor may use stolen credit cards to purchase products on your website. Before you know it, you've exceeded the payment processor's risk threshold, and they'll have no choice but to shut down the account automatically. This example highlights why you should always have a backup plan. If you are using Stripe, make sure that PayPal or some other payment processing service is active so that you can easily switch over without interrupting your business or needing to scramble.

As you scale your business, you'll attract more attention, which will make you a new target for security breaches, ransomware threats, and distributed denial-of-service (DDOS) attacks. Make sure that all of your software is current with the latest updates and fixes. Create periodic and offline backups. Ensure that your web hosting provider can prevent DDOS attacks.

Lastly, diversify your revenue sources. If you decide to sell your business after scaling it to a certain level, having a few big-spending customers will not favor potential buyers. As much as possible, avoid having single customers that account for more than 10-20% of revenue. You can find more details about selling your business in the next book in this trilogy, *Sell an Automated Online Business: Maximizing the Selling Price.*

For example, if governments account for 25% of your company's total revenue, try to increase the income from other segments to keep the ratio in check. If that is not possible, see if you can establish long-term contracts with varying renewal dates. Perhaps you can have the right mix of clients from various levels of government (municipal, regional, state, federal, and military), nongovernmental organizations (NGOs), and government corporations (UNICOR, AMTRAK, USPS, etc.).

Likewise, if your product is business-to-business (B2B), try to avoid having one Fortune 100 company account for more than 20% of your total revenue. Perhaps you can lock them into a long-term contract or some other creative solutions to help minimize the risk. If most of your customers are in one sector, find customers in other sectors. If you need to license a technology, see if others can supply a comparable technology. If most of your customers are in the US, find customers from other parts of the world. The bottom line is you will not turn down a big order from a big buyer. However, it's always good to be deliberate in finding ways to diversify your customer base, seeking out a range of customers.

CHAPTER 3

FOCUS ON CUSTOMER LIFETIME VALUE

Consider three overarching concepts: customer lifetime value (CLV), loss leaders, and customer acquisition cost (CAC). The CLV helps predict the overall net profit during the entire customer's relationship with the business. Wrapping it are loss leaders (a pricing strategy) and CAC.

If you spend $25 on Facebook ads to acquire each customer and that customer ends up buying a $100 online course, you've just made a $75 gross profit. So, the CAC is $25 or 25%. After purchasing the online course, the same customer signs up for a $20 per month subscription over the next 12 months (total sales of $240) and never purchases anything else after that; then, you've made $340 from that customer. The CLV of $340 for that customer came from the initial CAC investment of $25.

Essentially, up to an absolute maximum, you can continue to spend $25 to acquire each customer, and you'll continue to make $100 for the online course and expect some of them to pay the $20 monthly subscription over the next 12 months. You can't expect the CLV always to be $340 for every customer because some of them may not buy the monthly subscription, and some may buy it but cancel after six months or continue for up to 18 months. Eventually, as you collect more data, you'll be able to arrive at the average CAC and CLV amounts for your business.

What if it costs you $110 to acquire one customer? It means that the $100 online course is a loss leader. You will be losing $10 for every sale. However, if you know that they will eventually sign up for a monthly subscription, this may be an acceptable strategy as long as the total CLV far exceeds that CAC, keeping in mind the Rule of ⅓.

The loss leader pricing strategy is not new. In the 1970s, record companies used to sell sampler compilation albums of singles, B-sides, and obscure tracks. They sell these songs at significantly reduced prices hoping that listeners will discover an unknown artist or an unpopular song and eventually buy an entire album from that artist.

Chevrolet intentionally introduced Corvette as a loss leader in the 1950s. They thought that men would go to showrooms to look for the "automotive Playboy Bunny" car, which they cannot afford, and then end up walking away with a lower-priced vehicle. To their surprise, it had a different effect. It turned out to be a very profitable product and continued to perform well into the 1960s.

The same concepts apply today. Some manufacturers sell mobile phones and electronic devices as loss leaders. Still, they make up the revenue in subscription fees or higher profit accessories such as phone cases, headphones, charging stations, etc. Some printers are given away for free or sold at a low price, and they make money by selling refillable ink.

With automated online businesses, you see these three concepts (CLV, CAC, and loss leader) at play all the time. You will get a free download or access. Later on, the vendor will ask you to sign up for a paid subscription or purchase a product. Regardless, the sellers estimated their CLVs based on crude heuristics or predictive analytics. Depending on the technique that they used, the accuracy and sophistication may vary. However, it's essential to factor in these concepts when you are growing your business.

Depending on the industry, remember that acquiring new customers can cost up to five times more than retaining existing customers. Keeping even 5% of your customers can translate into an additional 25-95% in profit. You'll also have a higher success rate of selling to existing customers, 60-70%, compared to 5-20% for new customers. As such, incorporate upsells, cross-sells, and recurring revenue streams into your product and pricing strategies.

Introduce upsell and cross-sell

A well-known polyglot sells an online course for $197 to teach people how to pronounce the elemental sounds. Unbeknownst to most native speakers, English has 42 elementary sounds. By stringing these essential sounds together, along with the rhythm, intonation, volume, and other variables, we're able to produce words and sentences.

We make these elemental sounds depending on where we place our tongue, open our mouth, and several other factors. While we were growing up, we learned how to listen to our parents and naturally repeat the same sounds. Unless you get that good at making these sounds, you will not "hear" these sounds. As a result, you will not understand the language when someone speaks it, and you will not be understood when you talk.

In contrast, Spanish has 39, and French has 38 elemental sounds. Some of these elemental sounds overlap with English, so Spanish and French speakers can produce them without any difficulties. However, there are elemental sounds that are not available to other languages. As such, they need to practice with their mouth on how to produce these sounds. Otherwise, they will have a thick accent, and native speakers will not understand them. Spanish speakers tend to pronounce "breakfast" as "brefas," "teeth" as "teet," "ship" as "sheep" and so on. For French speakers, they pronounce "thorough and through" as "fuh-ruh and froo" because the sound "th" doesn't exist in French.

Anyway, this polyglot created online courses for several languages to teach these elemental sounds. Because most language learners or wanna-be polyglots tend to study more than one language, he upsells them for $97 to access the entire library. This offer is only available immediately after you purchase the first $197 product. If you buy each language course individually, you'll need to pay $197 each, so the $97 upsell is a great bargain.

With this simple upsell strategy, the initial $197 purchase became a $294 purchase yielding a 49% bump in total revenue! Because it is an online course, there was no incremental cost to the seller. It's pure profit.

If you buy a digital camera from an electronics store, the salesperson may suggest a memory card. That's cross-selling. Amazon generates 35% in additional revenue with their "customers who bought this item also bought" and "frequently bought together" features. The best time to introduce upsells and cross-sells is right after a customer completes the initial purchase. However, you can also present the offer through a welcome or confirmation email. Regardless of how you position it, look for opportunities to incorporate upsells and cross-sells with your current products.

Develop recurring revenue streams

If you can consistently sell a certain number of digital products per month (software, ebooks, audio files, games, photos, videos, plug-ins, etc.), you have a great business. From our previous example, you'll need to continue to spend $25 on Facebook ads to generate $100 in revenue. It's not a flawed model. However, you will need to start from zero every month.

What if a portion of your revenue is recurring? Then you have essentially diversified your income (some are one-time purchases and some are monthly subscriptions) while further enhancing your revenue predictability. In his book, *The Automatic Customer: Creating a Subscription Business in Any Industry*, John Warrillow presented nine subscription models, summarized below.

A membership website model offers access to content that is not available to the public. If you have become an Instagram influencer with millions of followers, people may subscribe to your online library of strategies and tactics to learn how you did it. While ancestry.com can be considered a membership website model, it is also an all-you-can-eat library model similar to the polyglot's previous upsell model. However, the polyglot decided to make the latter a one-time upsell instead of a monthly subscription. A monthly subscription might have been a better model, but it all depends on the data. As such, this scenario might be a great candidate for A/B testing.

The private club model provides access to something that is in limited supply and projects an image of exclusivity. Several YouTube influencers offer membership subscriptions using Patreon. "Patrons" pay a monthly subscription in exchange for exclusive rewards and perks from the content creators. Similar to the private club model, some software companies use the front-of-the-line model to offer tiered subscriptions to access their help desk. For example, customers on the lowest tier may only get email support, while those on the higher levels will have access to phone support with a promise to resolve their issues within 24 hours.

The consumables model works well for something that naturally runs out and can prove to be a hassle to replenish. Razors and diapers are examples of this model. If you sell dog toys or succulent plants online, the surprise-in-a-box model might work well for your business. WhatsApp and Airbnb used the network model. The more members they have in the network, the more valuable it becomes. WhatsApp's initial plan was to charge a $1 per year subscription. It sounds small, but with 2 billion users and 1.6 billion use it daily, the numbers quickly add up. However, Facebook decided to offer it for free after buying the app. Although Airbnb doesn't charge a membership fee per se, they make money on service fees.

The simplifier model and peace-of-mind model are almost the same. You can run a website selling monthly mowing service during the summer months and snow plowing service during the winter months. After a customer places an order, you can contract out the actual work to a local landscaping company. While you have them as a customer, you can also sell a home maintenance plan to open and close their pool, replace the filters on their furnace, check the water heater, replace the lightbulbs, and clean the windows. They pay a monthly subscription, and you make sure that your company or contractors complete the tasks. These are examples of simple automated online businesses that can quickly scale with the monthly subscriptions' predictable revenue.

Provide superior customer service

Your online business must provide superior customer service. Focus on having conversations with your customers instead of segmenting their support requests by channel such as email, chat, call, and others. While your main objective is to provide superior customer service, use the interaction as an opportunity to capture the net promoter score (NPS), which will be discussed later in this book. Leverage these customer service interactions to build your company's social proof. If they say something positive on one of their replies to a help desk ticket, ask for permission to use it as a quotation. You should also encourage them to write an online review.

Provide opportunities for customers to help themselves. As you receive support tickets, look for patterns and compile a frequently asked questions (FAQ) list. Use the FAQ as a filter so they can try to find an answer on their own before reaching out to your company's support team. If applicable, you can also include the FAQ in your welcome or onboarding emails. Most customers are happy to find help quickly on their own, and you'll end up responding to fewer support tickets. For repetitive tasks and replies, create a macro to save time and to provide consistent messaging.

The ticketing system should enable tracking, prioritizing, and solving customer support tickets all in one place. Live chat creates a personal connection with customers looking for fast and practical support. You can also incorporate social messaging to manage tweets and messages in one place. Lastly, phone support offers immediate and personalized solutions to complex issues. Make sure that your customer service software can support these features.

Turn customers into cheerleaders

As discussed in the previous sections, you'll need to nurture and build your company's social proof. Make this part of every process. Capture case studies, quotations, and reviews with every customer interaction.

In essence, you are turning your customers into passive cheerleaders for your business. Fortunately, you can turn them into active cheerleaders, too, by asking them to tell their friends. You can do this by creating marketing materials that they can easily share via email or social media.

If you want to formalize your business's "active" cheerleading process, you can also create an affiliate program. By turning your customers into affiliates, they'll get a commission for every sale they refer to you. Set all of these up automatically.

For example, they'd get an email invitation to sign up. After that, they can share the link to their friends, post it on a blog, or provide a link on a video. If someone clicks the link and eventually purchases a product, the affiliate marketing software will keep track of the commission and remit the referral fee, usually on a monthly cycle. The next chapter will discuss affiliate marketing in more detail.

★ ★ ★ ★ ★

You have read this far. That's great!

If you think this book deserves a five-star review, can you please post your comments on Amazon to let others know?

If not, please contact me at https://johnestrella, and I'll do my best to address your feedback so that we can make this book better.

—John

CHAPTER 4

CREATE A MARKETING WAR CHEST

To grow your online business, you need to sell more of the same product to more people. The key phrase is the "same product" because you need to increase the sales volume. With proper market positioning, you can sell the same product at a higher price. Besides, as discussed previously, there are also upsell and cross-sell opportunities. After all of these options have been exhausted, you can try to look for other channels to attract "more people" to your product.

If you have only been relying on word-of-mouth and organic search engine results to generate sales, you might be ready to introduce SEO. Explore content marketing, then CRO, then affiliate marketing, then influencer marketing, then native advertising, push notification, and so on, not necessarily in that order.

There are so many channels to explore, and you need to exhaust all of them before switching your focus to something else.

Only when you reach a saturation point where you can no longer grow your sales should you consider introducing a new product. It requires significant investment to create a new product and develop related marketing materials. As such, focus only on one product and build a sizable marketing war chest for it.

What should you include in a marketing war chest? Large organizations spend millions and billions of dollars on their marketing efforts. It is easy for a small online business to get carried away with "busy work," such as posting on social media with no measurable return on investment. Instead, come up with the minimum war chest and only add components as the needs arise. At a high-level, there are four key components: brand guidelines, digital assets, landing pages, and follow-up sequences.

Define the brand guidelines

When defining your brand guidelines, consider logo, tone, and experience. The logo has three elements: the brand mark, the brand name, and the strapline or tagline. For the tone, ensure that it reflects your brand's personality. A component of experiential marketing, the brand experience incorporates a comprehensive set of factors designed by the company to deliberately influence customers' feelings when interacting with your company or product.

You may already have an existing logo, so ensure that the brand mark depicts its proper place in the market. Social media try to have a brand mark that will fit nicely and fully inside a circle or a square. Most social media brands are of this shape, and you want to ensure consistent look-and-feel. The brand name is the trading name of the company or product. It must be legible in small and large font sizes. Lastly, the tagline displays a short phrase, in a smaller font, to add context to the brand name.

The colors and fonts for the logo are critical. When working with a graphic designer, make sure to designate a primary color, a secondary color, dark color, and light color, and consider both color and black and white treatments. The logo typically dictates the primary and secondary colors. The dark and light colors can be used as accents to sharpen the typography on the website, images, documents, and other marketing materials. For the font, adhere to the concepts of font pairing — select complementary primary and secondary fonts. The graphic designer defines the weight (regular or bold) and tracking (horizontal spacing between characters). As much as possible, stick to these four colors and two fonts to project a professional image.

While reflecting the brand's personality, the brand tone must connect with the audience and differentiate you from your competitors. The style may vary slightly depending on the audience, media, and goal. Regardless, it must be consistent to build connections, establish trust, increase revenue, and create a memorable brand. Research your target audience to know who they are and which media they consume (blogs, chats, videos, magazines, etc.). Take the time to analyze how your target audience interacts with each other online and offline. Ask them how they see your brand. Communicate your brand's values by succinctly and clearly describing who you are, and most importantly, who you are not, and who you would like to be. After that, audit your current marketing assets. Is it funny or serious, formal or casual, respectful or irreverent, enthusiastic or factual? Based on your findings, define your brand's tone and use it consistently in all of your communications.

The brand experience rounds the three components of a brand guideline. Some categorize the brand experience based on five personality dimensions (sincerity, excitement, competence, sophistication, and ruggedness). In contrast, others offer 12 brand archetypes (innocent, everyman, hero, outlaw, explorer, creator, ruler, magician, lover, caregiver, jester, and sage). Coca-Cola likes to inspire happiness. Amazon thrives on quick delivery of online products. Nike sells high-quality and fashionable athletic wear. Select your desired brand experience and incorporate it into all aspects of your marketing campaigns.

Develop digital assets

With adequately defined brand guidelines, it's easier to create digital assets. Your digital marketing assets will incorporate the brand logo, tone, and brand experience when building your marketing war chest. Marketing assets may include lists (customers, visitors, competitors, and keywords), texts (titles, captions, descriptions, and CTAs) and media (images, sounds, and videos), and guidelines (best practices, image dimensions, and restrictions).

Because you already have a thriving business, you likely have a list of customers. Use your customer list to grow your business by finding similar potential customers with comparable demographics and behaviors. Luckily, most digital platforms make it easier to capitalize on your current customer list. For example, Facebook allows advertisers to upload a list of customers with their name, email, phone, and address. While maintaining privacy, Facebook can use that information to find lookalike audiences. With a big enough customer list and a sufficient number of conversions (e.g., clicks, downloads, or purchases), the Facebook algorithm can get quite good at finding similar audiences with pinpoint accuracy.

Similarly, Facebook and Google can identify your website visitors, and you can retarget or remarket to them to come back to the website and make a purchase. With their extensive third-party advertising networks, you can have ads "follow" your prospective customers across the Internet or devices. For example, after visiting your website, you can display ads to potential customers on Facebook or on articles of a third-party blog that subscribes to Google's ad network.

Using Google Analytics or Google Search Console, you can identify the keywords your potential customers are using to find your company or product. Other tools, such as SEMrush allows you to gather intel about your competitors. Find out how you rank relative to your competitors, what ads they are running, and more. These keywords will allow you to build SEO and pay-per-click (PPC) strategies to bring more traffic to your website.

When building your digital assets, identify paid ad titles, captions, descriptions, and call-to-actions that your competitors use in their ads. Establish a disciplined approach to deliberately test the combinations and permutations of these texts for yourself using A/B testing. After you find a champion, continue to run A/B tests by introducing a challenger. You don't want to disrupt a well-performing sales funnel, but you can always split the traffic by sending a smaller portion to the challenger, e.g., 90% traffic to the champion and 10% to the challenger. If you want to achieve a specific milestone, you can increase the distribution accordingly, e.g., 80/20 or 60/40 split. Develop a list of challengers for your digital assets.

Creating media can get expensive quickly, especially if you need to create videos instead of still images. Start with four image variations to attract customers using a combination of positive and negative images, male and female, and something unusual with the sole purpose of getting attention. When you run A/B tests against these images, a champion will eventually emerge. As discussed previously, keep introducing a challenger to see if it can beat the champ.

For people who are already familiar with your company or product (existing customers or previous website visitors), create another set of four retargeting or remarketing images. Mix them up by highlighting the benefits, incorporating social proof (ratings and testimonials), case studies (before and after), and objection handling (e.g., refund guarantee, problem resolution).

Having eight images doesn't sound a lot (four attraction images and four retargeting or remarketing images). Still, if you factor in the number of ad placements, you'll end up with several dimensions for each. Resist the temptation to be lazy by using the same size for various ad placements. For example, an image that looks great on a desktop may not look appealing on a mobile device. There are slight variations on how Facebook, Instagram, and Messenger display ads. There are also varying limitations when rendering ads on a feed, marketplace, right column, inbox, and other placements. Make sure that you have the right size for each. After you have mastered the images, you can apply the same diligence and discipline to your video assets.

The guidelines from various marketing channels will dictate how to assemble all of these marketing assets into a coherent marketing campaign. Ensure that the entire campaign adheres to best practices and channel-specific restrictions. Failure to adhere to guidelines such as the ratio of image vs. text, prohibitive images, or questionable claims can get your ads canceled by the advertising platform. In some cases, the ad platform can shut down the entire account.

Streamline the landing pages

Digital businesses use various techniques to attract customers, such as SEO, paid ads, and affiliate marketing. Eventually, this website traffic will arrive at a landing page as "cold" or "warm" visitors. Regardless, wherever they came from before arriving on the landing page, the messaging and look-and-feel must be congruent. Meaning, if they were searching for "backpacking stove" on Google or they clicked on an ad with a picture of a backpacker cooking a meal with a mesmerizing background of a pristine river near snow-capped mountains on Facebook, the landing page must project the same image. Otherwise, the website visitor will just click away.

The critical distinction between cold and warm traffic is their state of mind when they arrive on the landing page. When someone is scrolling through pictures of dogs or cats on Facebook, they do not think about buying a backpacking stove. However, due to proper ad targeting, they see it because Facebook considers them active outdoors. They might have liked the Facebook Page of an outdoor store or an adventure travel company. In contrast, someone who is actively searching for backpacking stoves on Google already knows that she requires it. She's perhaps just looking for more information or ready to buy it. For warm traffic, there is an element of intent. Someone who typed "backpacking stove" might be looking for general information, but someone who searched for "best lightweight backpacking stove" is likely further along in the buying journey. So, the landing page must cater to the state of mind and the buyer's intent.

For cold traffic, there is an opportunity to educate them in the ad copy by highlighting the benefits, sharing social proof, and handling objections proactively. Assuming that's successful, consider them as warm traffic by adjusting the look-and-feel of your ads accordingly. However, remember that the ad's point is to catch their attention and get them to click. So, it's a balancing act between merely getting the click and qualifying them before they arrive on the landing page. It is not uncommon to separate these two functions. Get their attention and bring them as cold traffic and then retarget or remarket to them later as warm traffic.

Cold traffic should focus on helping visitors move along the customer journey. Introduce the brand and the product. Find out more about the visitors and capture their contact details so that you can follow-up with them. Brief online quizzes or simple assessment tools are low commitment tools that allow you to connect with the customers so that you can segment and qualify them.

Suppose you are selling a $5,000 product and your qualification process revealed their budget is about $100. In that case, you can try to close the gap by providing more information (encouraging prospective customers to adjust their budget) or disqualifying them outright. To narrow the gap, identify the problem they are trying to solve, present viable solutions, and set the high-level expectations (price ranges, benefits, features, delivery time, etc.). Retargeting and remarketing campaigns can then usher them along the customer journey because they have been "warmed up" as potential customers.

For warm traffic, highlight the benefits of your product and how it will solve their problem. Point out the "pleasures" they will experience and how they will eliminate their "pains." You need to present some social proof (reviews, quotations, case studies, etc.) and address their objections (will it also work for me, what if I don't like it, will I get support, etc.).

Initially, start with one cold landing page and one warm landing page and ensure your pages include all of a landing page's critical elements. Over time, you can develop additional variations depending on traffic sources, target audiences, and visitor behaviors. You can use the A/B testing approach by introducing a challenger to see if it can beat the champion with landing pages just as you did with ads.

Ensure that you are deliberate and systematic when performing A/B tests on the various parts of your landing pages. Be sure to test the main headline, supporting headline, unique selling proposition (USP), benefits of the offer, contextual images or video, social proof, reinforcement statement, closing argument, and call to action (CTA).

Establish follow-up sequences

We've touched briefly on retargeting or remarketing ads, which are essentially follow-up sequences. The attraction ad campaigns piqued their interest in your company or brand. Shortly after, they will start seeing follow-up ads to help them learn more about your product, come back to your website, and eventually buy your product. If they provided you with their email address or cell phone number, you could introduce automated follow-up sequences through those channels as well.

As an example, an online coach captures prospective customers' names, email addresses, and cell phone numbers before watching an automated on-demand webinar. At the end of the webinar, a CTA will ask them to book a call to discuss their needs. The booking page will use the email address to confirm the booking. An automated process will send follow-up text messages at 24 hours, one hour, and 15 minutes before the call to ensure that the potential customer will be on the phone when the coach calls. There may also be an option for what's called a voicemail drop. It's a ringless call that automatically deposits a pre-recorded voicemail to the prospective customer's cell phone to start nurturing the connection.

Most digital marketers use email as one of the elements of their follow-up sequences. Start with 3-5 emails. Try to spread them out and deliver them within 28 days. The 28-day or one month period is very specific because this will allow you to link a sale to a particular paid ad campaign. For example, if they clicked on a paid ad (day 1), they may click on a retargeting or marketing ad the next day. If they provide you with their email address at that point, the first email, a welcome message will be sent (day 2). From there, you can send follow-up emails 2 to 5 on days 3, 5, 7, and 14, respectively.

The cadence and aggressiveness will vary depending on what you are selling. Some products may require a longer sales cycle than others (e.g., 6-12 months) but try your best to narrow the sales cycle as much as possible so that you can directly correlate paid ads to actual purchases, helping you analyze your KPIs.

The first email in the sequence may simply introduce your company, brand, or product. The second email can discuss the benefits of your product. The third email can magnify the fear of missing out (FOMO). What is the prospective customer missing by not having your product? The fourth email can potentially share social proof, present case studies, and handle objections. If they haven't bought yet, the fifth email can be a bit aggressive by asking, "Have you solved your problem yet?" Somewhere in between, they may unsubscribe or decide to remain on the mailing list. If the latter, continue to send useful emails based on a regular cadence (weekly or monthly).

In all cases, make the follow-up sequences (paid ads, SMS, or emails) focused on them and how their lives will improve after they purchase your product. Write your emails to them as if you are having a conversation with a friend while ensuring that you stay true to the tone you defined in your brand guidelines.

CHAPTER 5

BUILD TRUST TO INCREASE CONVERSION

In overly simplistic terms, generating a profit is as simple as finding people to buy your products. As long as you can sell your products for more than the cost of making and selling them, you will generate profits. If you want to increase your earnings, you need to find more people to buy your products. Alternatively, you can sell the same products at a higher price. If you want to make even more profits, you can reduce the overall cost of producing your products. If you combine these three methods—finding more customers, increasing the price, and reducing production costs—you'll end up with a highly profitable business.

However, benefiting from these three methods are predicated on having your business affairs in order. That's why we talked about fully understanding the value chain at the beginning of this book. It is imperative to optimize the end-to-end processes because an inefficient operation will get magnified when you scale your business. Clumsy methods might be manageable when your business pace is slow and could become complete chaos when you increase the business volume. Accordingly, the focus should always be on the customer's lifetime value, a lifelong relationship, not a one-off transaction. As such, your marketing war chest must present a consistent brand promise and fully deliver against it.

With the foundation of a scalable, automated online business almost in place, we have one more step left to make it easier and faster to convert strangers into customers: It's all about effectiveness and efficiency. Along the customer journey, we need to build trust so that we can increase the conversion rates. To do so, you need to incorporate and highlight social proof, capture net promoter score (NPS), collect Google reviews, and gather Facebook reviews.

Incorporate and highlight social proof

Social proof, a psychological and social phenomenon, encourages prospective customers to copy others' actions and make them behave like your other customers in the same situation. Within a digital business context, you might be encouraging them to subscribe to a newsletter, sign up for a free trial, or buy a product online.

If someone is unsure whether to buy your product or not, they look to others for guidance, thinking others might know more about the current situation. People have a natural tendency to conform, so they look for reasons to legitimize their decisions in uncertain conditions. A straightforward example of this is looking at restaurant reviews to help decide where to go for dinner. Using social proof, you'll minimize or remove obstacles that may prevent them from purchasing your product.

Start by getting a "stamp of approval" from a credible third-party. These endorsements can come in the form of a formal certification such as registered education provider, authorized training partner, FDA approved, certified distributor, approved supplier, accredited licensee, Amazon bestseller, and so on. If your company got featured in local or national media, share it on your website. An interview, quote, or article on

Harvard Business Review, Huffington Post, CNN, or Fast Company will go a long way.

Celebrity endorsements can also help with social proof. There are formal ways to get one, and if done poorly, it can get expensive quickly. An alternative method is to reach out to a relevant celebrity via social media and see if they will give you a shout out on Twitter or YouTube, or share a post on Facebook, Instagram, and other social media channels. You can also accomplish the result through association: get and share a picture or video of someone famous talking about or using your product.

Although third-party approvals and celebrity endorsements can elevate your brand's social proof, do not underestimate the power of user testimonials. You've seen them on Amazon, Yelp, Tripadvisor, IMDb, Trustpilot, and other review websites. Your prospective customers need to see how people, just like them, use your product to solve their problems. Because different people view these reviews differently, make sure to offer multiple angles. Show them the before and after, demonstrate how your product benefited the customer, point out what they had to deal with before purchasing your product, directly address how your current customers overcame their doubts before purchasing your product, and so on. Later in this chapter, we'll cover how to incorporate collecting user reviews as part of your daily process.

We already discussed people's tendency to follow the crowd, so encourage them to do that. For example, Netflix, YouTube, and Twitter point out what's trending. For most people, instead of trying to figure out what to watch or follow, they conveniently just follow the crowd. As discussed earlier, Amazon has a feature called "frequently bought together." When you are browsing Product A, it may suggest that you also buy Product B. Presented in a slightly different way, there is another Amazon feature called "customers who bought this item also bought."

And of course, social proof will not be complete without word-of-mouth from friends and family. We have an inherent trust in people we already know, and Facebook does a great job of using this social proof. When you view a page, you can see which of your friends already liked it, and there is a convenient button next to it to allow you to invite your other friends. When you view a post, you'll see the engagements, comments, and shares. If you see a post with significant social proof, you tend to pause to check it out. That's social proof in action!

Capture net promoter score (NPS)

The net promoter score (NPS) allows you to measure the number of customers likely to recommend your product to someone else. On a scale of 0 to 10, it divides their ratings into detractors (6 or below), neutral (7 or 8), and promoters (9 or 10). Ask a straightforward question: How likely is it that you would recommend our company/product/service to a friend or colleague?

If your product has a steep learning curve, capture the NPS at the beginning of the customer journey and check with them again after fully realizing your product's benefits. If your product can deliver the results immediately, ask for the NPS shortly after. You may want to reach out to customers who gave a score of 6 or below. Find out what they didn't like and make sure to address their issues right away. For those who scored 7 or 8, ask them what your company can do better to improve. Have a conversation with those who gave a score of 9 or 10. What is it that they like? Make sure to ask for a testimonial and send them a link to your company's online review. These are the people helping to build your social proof and potentially referring you to their friends and family.

The NPS can range from -100 (all respondents are detractors) to 100 (all respondents are promoters).

Neutral or passives are not factored in the calculation. Calculate the percentage of promoters and subtract from it the percentage of detractors to arrive at the NPS. The benchmark varies across industries, so determine your baseline NPS and continuously find ways to satisfy your customers to improve the NPS over time.

Collect Google reviews

Google indicates that "Reviews on Google provide valuable information about your business to both you and your customers. Business reviews appear next to your listing in Maps and Search, and can help your business stand out on Google." We already know that reviews help build your social proof, but they can also help your company become more visible when it shows up on Google Maps and make your listing stand out on Google Search results.

While social proof is essential, don't underestimate the impact of Google reviews on your SEO and pay-per-click (PPC) as well. Using Google Ads, Google may also display the reviews as part of the Seller Ratings Ad Extensions, which adds credibility to your ad, increasing the number of clicks while lowering the cost-per-click (CPC).

Encourage your customers to leave a review. As a business owner, make sure to verify your business on Google My Business™. Doing so will make your information eligible to appear on Maps, Search, and other Google services. As a verified business, you can respond to reviews.

If you do not have many customers yet, focus on one platform initially, either Google or Facebook, depending on your customers' journey from initial contact to purchase. Google Analytics has an attribution feature that shows the conversion path, from the first touchpoint when someone visited your website to the point when they buy. If you notice that most of your customers arrive on your website using organic search, collect Google reviews to get the first 20-25 reviews. After that, switch your process and direct your customers to Facebook reviews until you have 20-25 reviews. Depending on how you want to distribute the reviews and the customers you are targeting, you may like to split your process equally to send 50% to Google and 50% to Facebook.

Gather Facebook reviews

Make sure that you have a Facebook Business Page so that you can collect reviews. You will also need it for running Facebook ads. To gather Facebook reviews, change the page settings by adding the Review Tab. After you turn it on, encourage your customers to check-in. As a significant side benefit, Facebook will automatically ask them to write a review when they check-in.

If you have a long list of customers, send an email and ask them to write a review. Better yet, make it an integral part of your process. You can do it at a convenient time along the customer journey. If NPS collection is already part of your strategy, do the same for Google and Facebook reviews. If you are getting plenty of likes on your business page's posts but not a lot of reviews, write a specific post requesting them to like your page, check-in, and write a review.

Similar to how Google uses Google reviews on their other products such as Search, Maps, Ads, and other services, it can also pick up Facebook reviews and display them on the search engine results pages (SERP).

CHAPTER 6

SCALE PAID DIGITAL ADVERTISING

There are several ways to increase revenue, but most of them take time, such as SEO, CRO, content marketing, affiliate marketing, and email marketing. Influencer marketing and viral marketing can generate a significant spike in sales, but they may not be sustainable in the long term. Traditional media can help too, but it's difficult to measure the direct effect of radio, television, newspaper, and magazine ads. Use a marketing channel with predictable sustainability that can be scaled quickly in a coordinated and controlled manner. This factor is where paid digital advertising shines.

It doesn't mean that you should ignore other digital and traditional marketing channels. Keep them going because they are part of the long-term strategy but allocate more resources to paid digital advertising. Even in this space, there are also multiple players. While Google Ads and Facebook Ads are leaders, Amazon Advertising is noticeably chipping away for a market share. Google offers access to YouTube, Gmail, and Blogger ads, and Facebook displays ads on Instagram and Messenger.

Other players include Microsoft Advertising (Bing, Yahoo, and AOL), Quora (question and answer platform), AdRoll (AI predictions of shopper's intent), Outbrain and Taboola (native advertising platforms), and Reddit (user-generated content). Depending on your target customer, you may also want to run paid ads on LinkedIn (B2B space), Pinterest (image marketing), Snapchat (younger audience), or TikTok (16-24 years old).

Follow the general strategy of leveraging existing customer data in your marketing campaigns. Potential customers who use Google to search for relevant keywords are warm leads. They know that they have a problem. They are looking for a solution to that problem. Your job is to usher them along the customer journey to purchase your product. So, make sure that you have paid ads running on Google. Along with that, start engaging Facebook users who expressed an interest in your work (e.g., project management), meet a particular life event (e.g., birthday), or exhibit a specific behavior (e.g., small business owner). After you have attracted their attention by visiting your website, leverage the tracking pixel to retarget and remarket to them later.

Leverage existing customer data

One key element of paid advertising is audience targeting. Most organizations start with necessary demographic information such as location (city, state, or country), gender, and age. Sometimes, they may include other filters such as interest, behavior, and other factors. While this approach appears to be logical, it might be better to tell Google and Facebook to find customers similar to your existing customers. After all, isn't it better to display your ad to people who are similar to your current customers instead of the general public, albeit with some basic parameters?

Google and Facebook collect data points when someone performs a search, checks in to a location, celebrates a life event, clicks a link, likes a page, or shares a post. As such, they can predictably and reliably find matching potential customers. Even if the profiles match, they have an added layer of sophistication in their algorithms to discern those who are most likely to click compared to those who will most likely buy. This subtle distinction might appear trivial, but focusing on the latter can contribute significantly to your company's bottom line and its ability to scale quickly.

Google uses the term Customer Match, Facebook calls it Custom Audiences, and LinkedIn supports Match Audiences. Regardless of the different terms, the concept for custom audiences is the same. Based on your customer "identifiers" (name, email, phone, and address), they can determine if that profile matches one of their users. If so, you can directly target that individual or find people with similar demographics, habits, interests, and so on. From a privacy perspective, they hash the data (a cryptographic security method) before the match to obscure personally identifiable information.

Suppose you do not have a big enough customer list. You can also track your website visitors' behaviors based on pages visited, shopping cart abandoned, freebies downloaded, and purchases completed. To do so, install a code snippet on your website pages to create your custom audiences. Similar to custom audiences, they perform the same function.

From customer audiences, create lookalike audiences and target them with your ads. Use data from your existing customers and website visitors to help you scale your paid advertising faster instead of prospecting a broader target audience.

Start with Google Search

We have discussed the importance of fully understanding the customer journey. It is even more critical when it comes to running paid ads on Google Search. It's not just a matter of matching relevant keywords to your product. You need to meet your target audience at the right place and at the right time. Otherwise, they may click your ad but never buy your product.

To ensure that you'll get a conversion to usher them along their customer journey, group your campaigns based on TOFU, MOFU, and BOFU. These acronyms correspond to where they are on the marketing funnel: Top Of the FUnnel, Middle Of the FUnnel, and Bottom Of the FUnnel, respectively. Top of the funnel visitors are those who are looking for general information. They may or may not know how to describe the problem that they are trying to solve accurately. Middle of the funnel visitors may understand their situation and have some idea of which product will solve it. When they start using the bottom of the funnel keywords, they have a higher intent of purchasing a solution to solve their problem.

For example, someone who might be interested in becoming a pilot may use TOFU keywords such as "become a pilot," "pilot salary," or "pilot training." As such, your ad should match the keywords that they used, and the link will take them to a landing page on your website with corresponding information. After they land on your landing page, use a tracking pixel to allow remarketing ads to nurture and usher them to the next step, MOFU.

When they see a remarketing ad on the Google Network, it will address MOFU keywords, which are much narrower with better-refined qualifiers such as "become a commercial airline pilot," "private pilot certificate," "commercial pilot certificate," and so on. They may even search for specific providers such as "flight school near me" or "discover flight [city name]." Although remarketing ads may have directed them to your MOFU landing page, others may simply use these search terms directly because they have been researching it for a while, or someone encouraged them to start the process. From here, they will further narrow down their search by using BOFU keywords.

At this point, they are on the last step of the customer journey. They are ready to buy, so you need to convince them that your product is the best solution. Highlight the benefits, share reviews, and handle their objections. They may even use actual product names, so ensure that you are always running branded search ads (i.e., Blue Sky Flight School). Continuing with our flight school example, BOFU words may include "best flight schools," "top pilot academy," "product 1 vs. product 2", "provider X cost," and so on.

The cost-per-click (CPC) tends to be more expensive for BOFU and cheaper for TOFU. That's because BOFU is further along the customer journey. These potential customers are ready to buy. It may seem counterintuitive, but start your Google Search paid ads on BOFU keywords. The competition will be challenging, and it will be costly, but these visitors have a higher possibility of converting into a sale. As you see results, scale your ad spend slowly but deliberately until you get the point of diminishing return.

If you spend $100 and you can sell $300, that's good. If you double your budget to $200 and you see $550 in sales, that's still good. However, if you increase your budget to $1,000 per day and only see $1,500 in sales, you may need to scale back and start allocating more of your budget to MOFU keywords. You want to get to a point where you have full coverage of the customer journey, so your ads will eventually include all TOFU, MOFU, and BOFU keywords.

Resist the temptation to start another paid ad channel, e.g., Facebook Ads, until you have a good handle on your Google Ads. Remember that Google Ads attract warm leads. Facebook Ads will typically bring you cold leads unless you are running retargeting ads (to be discussed later). To summarize, identify prospective customers from warm to cold audiences. Specifically, for warm audiences, stagger your targeting from BOFU to MOFU and then TOFU before moving to cold audiences.

Engage Facebook users

You'll start your prospecting for potential customers using Facebook Ads. As discussed previously, this will generate cold visitor traffic because they are not actively looking for your product. They may be browsing posts about cats, discussing current events, or watching seal rescues in Namibia. Your goal is to define your advertising conversion objective for each ad to usher them along the customer journey similar to the TOFU, MOFU, and BOFU stages on Google Search.

As you move them through each stage, they will become warm visitors and eventually hot visitors ready to buy. This section focuses on managing cold traffic. Moving them along from cold to warm and warm to hot can be achieved using Facebook retargeting and Google remarketing, covered in the next section. Even if you are using custom or lookalike audiences, these visitors are still cold until they get to a point where they express an interest in your product and decide to take the next step, e.g., sign up for a free trial or download an eBook.

You have three general advertising goals: awareness, consideration, and conversion. Run awareness campaigns to help potential customers recognize your brand, identify a problem (e.g., retirement self-quiz), and pique their interest. At the same time, you can also consider ad campaigns, encouraging people to reach out to your business to get information or visit your website to schedule an appointment. Lastly, conversion campaigns encourage people to buy or take the next step in becoming a customer. Similar to TOFU, awareness campaigns tend to be cheaper. Likewise, conversion campaigns tend to be more expensive, like BOFU.

There is also the caveat that people who click may not necessarily buy. So, while you may successfully generate awareness, you still need to narrow down that audience by retargeting them for consideration and conversion. For now, let's focus on awareness campaigns. These ad campaigns increase people's awareness of your business, brand, product, or service. Accordingly, you'd like to reach as many people as possible as cheaply as possible.

With awareness in place and TOFU and MOFU addressed by Google, we can retarget and remarket to these website visitors provided that you have installed the tracking codes, as discussed previously.

Remarket to website visitors

Facebook calls it retargeting, and Google refers to it as remarketing. Because most website visitors will land on your website and leave without ever coming back, you need to meet them where they usually hang out. That's what retargeting and remarketing are.

For example, Google Search will display your ad if someone searches for "become a pilot." When they click it, they will land on your landing page, and the tracking code will keep track of their interactions. So, you may want to remarket to them to read a blog titled, "pros and cons of private vs. commercial pilot." When they go to Facebook, they may see a retargeting ad with a picture of a pilot flying a small airplane over a beautiful clear blue sky with a caption "Discovery flight for $200". As you can see, they are no longer in the TOFU or awareness stage. They are now moving along nicely in the customer journey towards MOFU and BOFU, or consideration and conversion.

Because Google owns YouTube and Blogger, and Facebook controls Instagram and Messenger, along with their extensive networks, you can display a video showing someone like them using your product and raving about it. These are all possible options with remarketing. All it takes is to install tracking codes on your website from paid ad platforms. Once that's in place, it's just a matter of running prospecting ads (TOFU or awareness) and remarketing ads to usher them to MOFU or consideration. Eventually, BOFU or conversion ads will close the sale.

In terms of budget, use the same approach for regular Google and Facebook ads. Watch out for diminishing results. One factor that's unique with remarketing ads, more so than traditional ads, is ad fatigue. You don't want to show your ads too many times, too frequently, to the same people. Remember that your remarketing audiences will be smaller than prospecting audiences, limiting your wiggle room to scale the ad budget.

CHAPTER 7

INCORPORATE AFFILIATE MARKETING

Affiliate marketing should be a part of the marketing mix of any automated online business. Although it is a long-term strategy similar to SEO and CRO, affiliate marketing can generate a steady flow of qualified traffic to your website after establishing it correctly. Unlike SEO and CRO, where it is difficult to attribute a particular sale to a source, sophisticated affiliate tracking software can distinguish whether an affiliate assisted on the first or last click along the customer's purchase journey.

While paid advertising can immediately generate results and be scaled quickly, the business owner must invest marketing dollars upfront. There is no guarantee that it will yield profitable results. In contrast, a business owner only needs to pay the affiliates after generating a sale using affiliate marketing. The affiliate carries most of the risks making affiliate marketing an attractive marketing channel. Additionally, if nurtured correctly, this can intrinsically and directly help with your SEO efforts. Each link from an affiliate is essentially a backlink that search engines use as one of the parameters for measuring a website's authority. Affiliates who present comparison and review pages also elevate the brand's social proof, making it easier and faster to close a sale.

To effectively leverage affiliate marketing, business owners should prepare an affiliate offer, recruit affiliate partners, address common issues, and engage an affiliate manager.

Prepare an affiliate offer

As a business owner, you need to convince your potential affiliates to partner with you. As such, it is imperative that they believe in what you are selling and that they will receive fair compensation for their effort. In general terms, they'd prefer to promote a $100 product with a 10% commission ($10) instead of a $5 product with a 20% commission ($1). While it might be easier to sell a lower-priced product, they'll need to sell a lot more to generate the same commission than a higher-priced product.

Regardless, you need to make the sign-up process simple and straightforward. After you approve the affiliates, make sure to onboard them swiftly and adequately by setting the expectations and providing them with your brand's marketing assets (logos, images, key messages, and so on). Clearly state whether you allow branded campaigns. That is if they can use your brand when they run their own paid advertising. If you are not running paid ads yet, you may allow them to do it. You can always cancel the privilege at a later time should you wish to do it in-house. Doing this enables your affiliates to take the next steps and become productive immediately while presenting your brand consistently across the online world.

If you follow the Rule of ⅓, you can pay up to 30-35% affiliate commission per sale. Some automated online business owners offer up to 50%, sometimes even higher, arguing that there is almost no cost to produce their product because they are selling digital products. Without the help of affiliates, potential customers will not be able to discover their products. While that argument is accurate, try to stick to the Rule of ⅓. Should you wish to offer more, put a time limit on it, for example, during the first 90 days of joining the affiliate program.

Start by offering 10% as a regular commission. Some prominent publishers may ask for more, and setting the standard commission at 10% allows you to extend a higher commission of 12% to 15%. For select campaigns (e.g., holidays), you can offer a commission of 20-25% per sale for a limited time. This structure will allow you to stay well below the Rule of ⅓ (30-35%), which means more profit for each sale.

After establishing the commission structure, define the attribution model. This model will depend on the affiliate tracking software. Some only support first clicks. Others only track the last click, and few offer weighted commission (e.g., 60% for the first click and 40% for the last click). Whether the attribution is first or last click is a fundamental distinction. Affiliates who focus on SEO and content marketing (e.g., best product or top product blog posts or videos) generate the first click to bring awareness to your brand. After prospective customers have found you, discount or coupon affiliates will help close the sale, thus the last click.

You also need to set a timeframe, that is, how much time can pass between the first click and the actual purchase to recognize the referral? This timeframe will vary depending on the product, sector, customer type (individual or business), and sales cycle length. It can be as short as 30 days or as long as 90 days. You also need to consider your company's refund policy, because you wouldn't want to pay the commission until after the refund period. Otherwise, you may end up paying a commission, and the customer may end up returning the product. So, if you set the time frame to 60 days and you allow up to 30 days for a refund, your affiliates may not get paid until after 90 days later. Clearly outline this timeline in the affiliate agreement.

Any good affiliate marketing software will have tracking and reporting. All of your website pages will need to embed a code snippet to enable this functionality. With the tracking code in place, you and your affiliates can generate reports to determine the number of clicks, conversions, total commissions, and total sales. With the affiliate offer in place, you can now turn your attention to recruiting affiliate partners.

Recruit affiliate partners

There are different types of affiliate partners, so where you find them and how you engage them may vary. Major broad categories include niche affiliates, conversion arbiters, discount websites, content farms, cart abandonment services, and organization partners. Regardless of the type, they have one common goal—to match their audience to your brand by providing a link to your website.

Niche affiliates are actively looking for products to promote to their audiences. They may have a mailing list, a niche website, a unique social media profile, or a famous video channel. They will occasionally share with their audience a link to your website. If their audience ends up buying your product, they'll get an affiliate commission for it.

Conversion arbiters may use SEO so that their landing page will rank high on BOFU search terms such as "best online accounting software," "top accounting software," "accounting software X vs. Y," and so on. Suppose you allow them to use branded terms (e.g., Company X, Company X reviews, Company X alternative, etc.). In that case, they may also search campaigns at their own expense, hoping that they can pocket the difference between the affiliate commission and their paid ad costs.

As the name implies, discount sites are just that, and they offer discounts or coupons from various vendors. They may also provide rebates to their members. Some business owners (often referred to as merchants within the affiliate marketing world) look down upon these affiliates because the discounts chip away from their profit. However, a discount is a powerful incentive because it can help close the sale. Merchants concerned about the impact of deals on their profit may offer a weighted commission (e.g., 80% for the first click and 20% for last-click affiliates). Discount sites are an essential element of the sales journey ecosystem, so you're best to embrace it.

Content farms create content such as blogs or videos on various topics. Because of the volume of content that they produce, they tend to rank higher on search engines. They are instrumental in discovering potential customers who you may not have thought of as potential customers. Some of them may also own several digital properties that cater to various topics and render on multiple platforms (desktop, mobile, app, native, notification, ad network, etc.).

Cart abandonment services tend to be different from other affiliates because they offer a specific benefit to recover lost revenue opportunities. In exchange for using their proprietary technology, they take a commission for each recovered sale. For example, when someone abandons their online shopping cart, a popup may appear, offering them a free trial or a discount coupon. Likewise, on exit intent (when someone moves their mouse away from the page and towards the back button, close button, or URL bar), a popup may appear to get them to stay. These services can also send follow-up emails until the prospective customer completes the purchase or opts out of the mailing list.

Organization partners are harder to recruit, but the volume of referrals that they can bring along with the credibility that your brand will receive because of their endorsement makes them extremely valuable as potential affiliates. Look for associations, organizations, and institutions and offer a unique discount code to their members. It's a win-win-win situation because their members benefit from the discount. The organization gets a commission for each sale, and your brand gets an endorsement and recruits a new customer.

Join an affiliate network as a merchant to start looking for affiliates. Find the best affiliate network that meets your needs based on setup costs, monthly fees, service fees, network size, community support, merchant and affiliate tools, and tracking and reporting capabilities. While it is possible to join multiple affiliate networks, it's best to focus and stick to only one. Otherwise, you can run into issues of paying one or more affiliates for the same sale. It can get complicated very quickly, and some of your affiliates may complain that you are cheating them with their commissions. This scenario is just one of the many issues you may encounter, and it's an excellent time to start talking about how to address common problems.

Address common issues

As discussed previously, you may run into duplicate commissions. To avoid it, run only one affiliate program. If you are currently running more than one, gradually work to consolidate them into a single network. Other issues that you need to address are refunds, reputation, and losing key affiliates.

You don't want to pay a commission to an affiliate if you will end up issuing a refund to a customer. Some unscrupulous affiliates may generate several fraudulent transactions to collect commissions. After you've paid the commission, the chargebacks and refunds will arrive, and you'll have no way to recover the paid commissions from the affiliates. Although most affiliate networks help block these fraudsters, you can add an extra layer of protection by not paying commissions until after the refund window, typically 30 days after purchase. After they help make a sale, they will have to wait for the next payment cycle 30 days after the sale.

It is also essential to maintain your brand's reputation. By appropriately onboarding your affiliates and providing them with your brand assets, you have proactively reduced this potential risk. However, you need to monitor how your affiliates represent your brand. Keep an eye on top-performing affiliates to confirm their content's accuracy and that everything is remaining aligned with your brand.

Although affiliate marketing helps with sales source diversification, you may still end up with a handful of high-performing affiliates. That's good news and bad news, mostly good news, because they contribute to a steady and continuous revenue flow. However, if they decide to leave as an affiliate, perhaps to push a competitor's product, you'll immediately see a significant impact on your bottom line. As with anything, make sure to maintain a healthy relationship with your affiliates. Continue to offer an attractive commission rate and optimize your conversion flow to increase sales.

Engage an affiliate manager

At some point, as you streamline your business processes, you may need to hire an affiliate manager to scale your affiliate program. Some individuals and agencies specialize in managing affiliate programs. They can help you with outreach to potential affiliates. They can also engage existing affiliates by sharing marketing calendars and promotional offers. Established affiliates have a marketing calendar, so you need to give them ample time to slot your requests into their calendars.

By having someone manage your affiliate network, you will also gain access to their partners. They possess significant industry expertise, so they can advise you about what will work best for your particular business. Affiliate marketing is a crucial element of evergreen traffic sources and a vital component of an automated online business. With your affiliate program in place, you can continue to invest in other evergreen traffic sources, so we'll discuss those other options in the next chapter.

★ ★ ★ ★ ★

If you still have questions that I haven't addressed so far, please don't hesitate to contact me at https://johnestrella.com.

If you haven't done so already, I'd greatly appreciate it if you can give this book a glowing review on Amazon. Thank you so much for your support!

CHAPTER **8**

INVEST IN EVERGREEN TRAFFIC SOURCES

Scaling an automated online business requires three foundational components. First, the entire value chain must be clear and measurable. Second, end-to-end processes must be highly optimized to minimize manual activities that can introduce unpredictable variability and maximize effective and efficient product delivery through automation. Third, decisions should focus on nurturing and increasing customer lifetime value. After the three foundational components are in place, baseline marketing assets can follow to lay the groundwork to grow the business rapidly.

Baseline marketing assets include creating your marketing war chest and building trust with customers to increase conversions. From here, paid digital advertising can accelerate sustainable growth. It's a short-term tactic because results are immediate. If something is not working, the business can pivot and try a different marketing campaign. If it does work, it becomes a critical element of the long-term marketing mix and affiliate marketing. These two channels alone can take a business to the next level. Additional tactics such as multiplying revenue via partnerships, enhancing backlinks quality and quantity, collaborating with other influencers, and increasing top-of-mind awareness will further accelerate its growth.

Multiply revenue via partnerships

Affiliate marketing tends to focus on building individual relationships with each affiliate. Although some affiliates are more prominent than others, it's still a one-to-one effort. As such, it steadily increases revenue and consistently contributes to a stream of customers. It's a one-time effort that continues to generate income, thus an evergreen traffic source.

In contrast, paid digital advertising requires constant input. If you invest a steady budget, you can expect to see a steady return on investment. Up to a certain point, if you spend more, you'll earn more. However, if you stop running digital ads, the revenue will stop also. That's why it's vital to add partnerships into the marketing mix. Partners can function similarly to affiliates (one time-effort, steady growth, and consistent revenue). A paid digital ad can yield consistent results, which means more inputs and higher outputs.

Will co-branding with a partner help increase revenue? Absolutely yes! As an example, using their shared value for extreme adventures, GoPro equipped action sports athletes to capture their races and stunts. Red Bull enjoys a reputation for sponsoring these events. By leveraging each other's strengths, the Red Bull Stratos Project presented a more substantial value to their fans. Kanye West partnered with Adidas to develop Yeezy, a high-end line of footwear. A co-branding effort between Taco Bell and Doritos resulted in Doritos Lacos Tacos, resulting in one billion units sold in its first year.

Distribution partnerships involve bundling or listing your product with a partner. If you have written a course, a global training provider can include your course in their catalog. If it's an online course, get it listed in an online learning portal. A professional association can provide an official product endorsement, and so on. With a distribution partnership, you can access their wider audience using either a commission or a royalty structure. With the former, the partner gets a commission for every sale, just like an affiliate. With the latter, they sell the product, and you get a royalty for each sale.

There are several other options for partnerships such as sponsorship, licensing, white labeling, loyalty, product placement, and more. They work in a traditional sense for brick-and-mortar companies such as AT&T Park in San Francisco, PNC Park in Pittsburgh, or the Rogers Centre in Toronto. It doesn't take that much effort to leverage them for an online business. GoDaddy's reseller program succinctly stated it as "your business, our products." They provide all the necessary tools to let resellers sell domains, hosting, email, website builder, and more directly on their website.

Enhance backlinks quality and quantity

Search engine marketing (SEM) generates traffic by increasing visibility in search engine results pages (SERPs), usually through paid advertising. Search engine optimization (SEO), a key element of SEM, leverages good content marketing to improve their SERP visibility and pay-per-click (PPC) initiatives.

Establish a manageable cadence to create white papers, infographics, videos, podcasts, webinars, and blog posts. To access a wider audience, consider co-creating these marketing assets with other content creators who share the same values. Your partners can create backlinks to improve your domain's authority. A portion of your marketing budget should be allocated for continuous link building to point back to the treasures inside your marketing war chest. Some individuals and agencies can perform these tasks on your company's behalf.

Collaborate with other influencers

Make sure that you have a thorough understanding of your target customers. Find out who influences their buying decisions. Armed with that information, narrow down the influencers who create content for your target audience. Go beyond the traditional social media influencers. Reach out to professional associations, online groups, and informal tribes who share the same passion for a product or a cause.

After you have identified your potential influencers, set your goals, what outcomes would you like to achieve with these influencers: awareness, consideration, or conversion? Unlike affiliate marketing, SEO, and PPC, influencer marketing requires a human touch, so you need to nurture that relationship. It's not a set-it-and-forget-it setup, but it's excellent to build social proof and increase top-of-mind awareness.

Increase top-of-mind awareness

Popular with TV and film, some agencies specialize only in product placement to help with top-of-mind awareness. This tactic plays on the psychological state of potential customers by increasing brand awareness and social proof.

In the online world, as an example, the same tactic can be replicated using awareness campaigns. Facebook supports paid ad campaign goals for brand awareness and reach. They will try to increase people's attention to your brand by showing your ad to as many people as possible within your target audience.

With the other marketing efforts discussed throughout this book, we have intrinsically addressed top-of-mind awareness. However, it's worthwhile to monitor it periodically and deliberately. You can survey your existing customers to find out how they first heard about your brand. If you randomly ask people about your brand, you'll be able to measure how many can recall your brand. You can also look at your website's traffic and assess the volume of branded search keywords. Incorporate social listening to see what others are saying about your brand. Measure the volume of mentions, reach, and engagement, and compare them to industry benchmarks.

These tools and techniques will help you scale your automated online business. Identify the entire value chain for your business, maximize the customer lifetime value (CLV), pull specific levers to increase revenue, and be strategic using social proof and conversion rate optimization.

As a reminder, it all starts with deconstructing the value chain to ensure your business has a solid foundation rooted in reliable data analytics and removing elements that block or inhibit scalability. Just as you successfully created and launched your automated online business, these are the key elements to help you scale effectively. Happy growing!

Index

Automated Online Business Books

Start an Automated Online Business: Turning Your Passions Into Millions

Paperback: 978-1-990135-00-2
Kindle: 978-1-990135-01-9
Audible: 978-1-990135-02-6

Scale an Automated Online Business: Unlocking and Perfecting Profitability

Paperback: 978-1-990135-03-3
Kindle: 978-1-990135-04-0
Audible: 978-1-990135-05-7

Sell an Automated Online Business: Maximizing the Selling Price

Paperback: 978-1-990135-06-4
Kindle: 978-1-990135-07-1
Audible: 978-1-990135-08-8

Solopreneur Programs

Apply to our programs by visiting our website.
https://agilitek.com/solopreneur